97 Ways to Make a Dog Smile

97 Ways to Make a Dog Smile

Jenny Langbehn

WORKMAN PUBLISHING · NEW YORK

Library of Congress Cataloging-in-Publication Data is available.

ISBN 978-0-7611-8448-5

Design by Jean-Marc Troadec

Photo research by Melissa Lucier

Workman books are available at special discounts
when purchased in bulk for premiums and sales promotions
as well as for fund-raising or educational use.
Special editions or book excerpts can also be created to specification.
For details, contact the Special Sales Director at the address below,
or send an email to specialmarkets@workman.com.

Workman Publishing Co., Inc.
225 Varick Street
New York, NY 10014-4381
workman.com

WORKMAN is a registered trademark of Workman Publishing Co., Inc.

Printed in China
First printing March 2015

10 9 8 7 6 5 4 3 2

Dedication

For two of the finest people ever to
grace the planet: my parents,
Pam and Roger. Through them I learned
the importance of respecting those who
can't necessarily speak for themselves.
They encourage me in all things,
and have never begrudged me the
occasional batch of orphaned creatures.
I love you both very much.

Introduction

Dogs are extraordinary creatures. Each has his or her own distinct personality; and like the proverbial snowflake, no two are just alike. Loyal and flirtatious, placid and rambunctious, ready for a marathon play session and then quietly and comfortably nestled on the sofa, they live to please and seem to do so with great joy. This drive to please is unique among animals; no other creature is so motivated by its guardian's happiness. And in the face of that kind of devotion, it's impossible to not want to reciprocate.

As all dog lovers know, dogs will delight in even the simplest activities. I find this one of their most enchanting and endearing qualities. Every walk is thrilling. Every car ride brings the possibility for adventure. Each rub is so pleasurable it simply must not end! Even a makeshift toy, like an old sock, can be extraordinarily fascinating each and every time it is played with. It is so easy and so much fun to make your dog happy—so happy that he or she actually smiles—that it makes the continuous mission to think up new and invigorating ways to please your pooch a natural extension of your love. The 97 ways suggested in these pages are just a few of the infinite possibilities for having fun.

The rubs, tickles, games, tricks, and treats that I include here are tried-and-true favorites that have worked for my own dogs, and many of the dogs that I have come to know over the years. I am pleased to report that many of my tricks of the trade have made the veterinary appointments of numerous dogs (and their people) that much more pleasant. (In fact, quite a few patients actually look forward to their visits!) Most activities developed from the simple act of diversion from an unpleasant procedure, and evolved into one of sheer fun and unadulterated joy. Of course, not every suggestion is right for every dog. Many factors like breed, temperament, and age will affect a dog's reaction. Pay close attention to any activity your dog is enthusiastic about, and skip anything that seems to make him or her uncomfortable.

My hope is that this book will be the springboard for a lifelong plan of creative and bonding exercises in fun for you and your dog. I would love to hear about your experiences with the activities in this book as well as any fun that results from them. Feel free to write me at doggiesmile@aol.com.

97 Ways to Make a Dog Smile

1

Lower-Ear Noogies

A tried-and-true massage location, the ears are very sensitive sites. At the base of the ear, gently rub your knuckles in true noogie fashion. (To make a noogie, form a half fist with your knuckles sticking out.)

2

Inner-Ear Noogies

Put your hand in noogie position, and with the knuckle of your middle finger, rub the little piece of cartilage that juts out at the entrance to your dog's ear. The dog's head will probably tilt to one side, with her eyes half-closed.

3

You are getting very sleepy . . .

Using your index finger, slowly stroke the bridge of the nose in the direction in which the hair grows.

4

Using both hands, gently knead (don't pinch!)

the excess skin of your dog's back and scruff. Sing a rousing rendition of "That's Amore" as you knead the dog's skin like pizza dough.

5

Make a "hand" sandwich.

When your dog is lying on his side, slip your hand between him and the floor (starting at the shoulder), and run your hand slowly along the length of his body. The ripple will result in canine ecstasy. Doggie will probably roll onto his back, which means you can do this again using both hands—one on each side.

NOTE: Try this with your foot if the dog doesn't mind foot pats.

6

The Jell-O Mold

For our portly friends, place one
hand (palms flat) on either side
of the dog's body and
gently shake the flesh.
Optional sound effects include:
a whirring noise or
the old Jell-O gelatin jingle
("Watch it wiggle, see it jiggle . . .").

7

The Thumper

Cupping your hand slightly,
use your fingertips to rapidly
scratch your dog on her side,
just where the ribs end.
Be prepared for the foot that may
involuntarily waggle and thump
in classic bunny fashion.

8

Locate all of the cowlicks

in the various places on your dog's coat, and trace them in a spiral motion with your index finger. Go with the grain for a soothing effect, against it to create shivers of excitement.

9

The Full-Body Massage

Starting at the snout, thoroughly and methodically massage the entire length of her body.

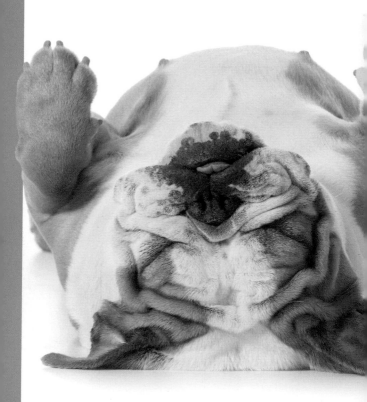

10

The White-Glove Massage

For a simple variation on more standard massages, try your usual process with a pair of socks on your hands. The sensation is quite different for the dog because you are covering much more surface area with each stroke, and because your hands look funny with socks on them.

11

Scratch under your dog's collar.

Most petting skips over this vital spot, but many dogs fall over in pure rapture when this area is addressed.

12

The Instant Face-Lift

Using the palms of both hands, smooth the skin of the cheeks gently back in stroking motions toward the neck. This action has been described as eliciting a "false grin," but I assure you that the smile is genuine.

NOTE: I like to accompany this move with commentary in my best Zsa-Zsa Gabor voice: "Dahlink, you look vanderful."

13

Dogs have very expressive eyebrows.

In some cases, the brows differ in color from the rest of the facial hair. These spots are extremely relaxing massage points. Rub the eyebrows gently in small circles, being careful not to poke the dog's eye.

14

El Matador

Some dogs love the romance and pageantry of a good old-fashioned bullfight. Wave a towel or blanket provocatively while shouting "Toro, Toro!" As your little hornless bull charges, whisk the "cape" away at the last second.

NOTE: If you have cheering audience members at your disposal, by all means employ them!

15

Do you miss your dog while you're away?

She misses you, too!
Phone home and play a message
on the speaker of your
answering machine.
Make sure you say her name
loud and clear.

16

Place your ear over your dog's chest so that you can hear his heartbeat.

In time to your
new canine metronome,
serenade him with the first song
that evolves from the beat.

FACT: "Duke of Earl" is by far
the most common selection.

17

Woof!

Most dogs are not fooled by a human's
imitation barks, but they are intrigued
by them. See how good your bark
(or bow-wow or howl) is by testing it on
your dog. If she barks back, you are truly
bilingual and the two of you can have
fascinating dialogues in her native tongue.
If she cocks her head and looks at you
like you landed from another planet,
stick to speaking English.

NOTE: This test is best performed in the privacy
of your own home to avoid neighbors' stares.

18

Learn to juggle.

Or better yet, how *not* to juggle.
For obvious reasons, a bad juggler
is a dog's best friend!

19

Have a night at the movies.

Play a nature video—specifically, a documentary about wolves. If he usually responds to TV, the sounds will inspire interest and possibly conversation with the wolves.

20

Form your own conga line.

Place your dog's paws on your waist and conga away!

NOTE: This is best for large dogs. Most smaller breeds prefer to dance solo.

21

The Name Game

Who doesn't love the sound
of her own name? Say your
dog's name over and over to her
(Is Maisie a good girl?
Yes, Maisie is very nice.) and
with fun variations (Maisie,
The Maiser, The Maisinator,
Miss Maiserina, Maiseroni).

22

Dogs love to outwit their people.

Pretend to unknowingly
drop a morsel of food
(preferably their own), and look
for the cat-that-ate-the-canary look
when your dog scoops it up.

NOTE: For our canines with a conscience, this could
prove torturous as they battle to resist temptation.

23

Joyride!

Hop in the car and take a
spin. Crack the windows
and let the wind stream
through the dog's ears and fur.
The windblown look is definitely
in this season.

24

Towel Time

Dry off a damp dog with a towel fresh from the dryer. A warm rubdown is toasty-good fun.

NOTE: Beware of static cling!

25

Give the dog a gift.

If everyone else is getting
a present—at gift-giving holidays,
for example—the dog should have
one, too. Otherwise it's not fair!
Most dogs are thoroughly
excited by the prospect of
their very own package.
Just make sure that she does
not ingest the wrapping
as well as the treat inside.

26

Play hide-and-seek.

Hide a treat in a clever spot and
see how long it takes for the dog
to discover it.

27

Play the "Which Hand" game

by hiding a treat in one of your clenched fists, and seeing if your dog will choose the correct hand.

NOTE: Resist the urge to tease your dog by hiding nothing in either hand. Your dog will not find this amusing.

28

Flying Saucers

Incorporate a little exercise
into treat time by tossing
miniature rice cakes (à la Frisbee)
for your dog to chase.
These low-calorie treats pack
a big crunch without padding
the waistline, and they are
fun to catch.

29

Do you want to go for a . . . WALK?!

Say this handy phrase, then repeat "A walk! A walk!" while dancing around in front of the door.

NOTE: You must actually go for a walk after you say this.

30

Flea Pockets

Scratch the small and seemingly superfluous flaps of skin located at the base of dogs' ears. Legend has it that these are the fissures in which fleas would retreat to sleep for the evening.

31

The Aunt Martha

For our jowl-endowed friends,
all of that copious skin just begs to
be pinched! Don't forget to say,
"You are just soooo cute!"
(And don't pinch too hard.)

32

The Three Little Bears Routine

If you are feeling particularly silly (and no one is looking), give your dog a huge surprise by letting her find you curled up in *her* bed for a change!

33

Puppy Pilates

If you do floor exercises or yoga at home, let your dog join you on the mat. Most dogs love to join in, especially for moves like Downward-Facing Dog.

34

"Holy ears, Batman!"

Did you know that your floppy-eared dog does a remarkable impression of a fruit bat? Simply lift both ears into the upright position. You'll be amazed by the transformation! When the ears are in superhero formation, it's time to play superheroes. Take turns being hero and villain.

NOTE: Some dogs are masters of disguise and can accomplish this feat on their own by lying on their backs.

35

Play catch.

Throw the ball; let the dog bring it back. A classic. Mix it up with pretend throws, which gets most dogs even more excited. (Just actually throw the ball every now and then.)

36

Freezie Chew

Soak a doggie rope toy in water,
and then freeze it.

NOTE: This is a great summertime treat that is also
ideal for teething puppies.

37

The Hansel and Gretel

Leave a trail of plain popped
popcorn around the house or yard.

38

Subliminal Game

Sneak a familiar word into a long rant. For example: "Today I was shopping in the supermarket, and I noticed that there was a spill in the condiment aisle **cookie** and it took nearly ten minutes for someone to clean it up...." You may be surprised how closely your dog actually listens to what you have to say.

NOTE: You must provide Doggie with whatever you have subliminally mentioned.

39

"Luke, I am your father."

Speak to your dog through the cardboard cylinder of a paper towel or wrapping-paper roll. Your dog will love your Darth Vader voice!

40

Do jumping jacks.

C'mon, everyone!
One, two! One, two!

41

Hot Dogs

Rub your pooch down with a cool, wet towel. Relief without the shock! Pay special attention to your dog's ears and feet. Cooling these spots in particular will guarantee canine comfort. *Ahhhhh!*

42

Swedish Massage

Very much like your usual massage routine, only brisker, this massage is performed to the beat of your dog's favorite ABBA tune!

NOTE: Most dogs enjoy "Dancing Queen."

43

Tickle the Ivories

Play your dog's ribs like a piano
keyboard. Sing along as you
practice your scales.

NOTE: Guitarists may find their dogs are built
for a similar effect, if a strumming motion is employed
across the ribs. This works particularly well in breeds
with snouts long enough for fingering.

44

The Ham Hock

For dogs that prefer a deep-tissue massage, knead those thigh muscles as though tenderizing your main course!

45

Scratch and Sniff

It's payback time for all that sniffing you get. The next time the dog sniffs you, sniff her back. Make it as loud and reciprocal as you can.

NOTE: As you may have witnessed, this behavior is perfectly acceptable in doggie social situations, and not at all considered rude. In fact, your dog may be touched that you made the gesture!

46

Rubbed the Wrong Way

Pet your pup *against* the grain.

47

Pregame Pep Talk

This massage is performed as your dog sits in front of you, using your thumbs to work the muscles around your dog's scapulas (shoulder blades). Great warm-up before any marathon ball or stick chasing. Go get 'em, champ!

48

Daddy Longlegs

Form your fingers into your best spider imitation and lightly massage your dog from head to toe. You may notice his skin crawling, but in a good way!

49

Wax On, Wax Off

For our Zen pooches, a methodical series of circular massage motions can induce a meditative state that brings doggie serenity!

50

The Treat Fairy

While your dog is asleep, attempt to sneak a treat under his pillow without disturbing him. Dogs love to wake up to a surprise!

51

Go, Speed Racer!

Make an obstacle course in your yard and race the dog through it. Again! And again!

NOTE: Remember that dogs are notorious cheaters.

52

Piñata

Fill a brown paper bag
with dog-friendly treats and toys.
Smack it open and watch
the sky rain Milk Bones.

53

The hills are alive . . .

It is a little-known fact that dogs love Julie Andrews (and, really, who doesn't?). Find the nearest hill or field, and with arms extended, twirl about as though you were high in the Austrian Alps.
If your dog is unimpressed, you can always yodel. This ups the excitement ante considerably.

54

Bring Your Dog to Work Day

What's more exciting than a day at the office? Nothing! New smells, new people. No wonder you go there all the time.

NOTE: Don't bother with W-2 forms or 401(k) plans, but frequent trips to the water cooler will be appreciated.

55

Top-Notch Massage

That bony peak atop your dog's head actually has a name: the nuchal crest. There is no real known purpose for the protuberance, but some more spiritual scholars postulate that it may be the dog's antennae for mystical energies, and should be massaged regularly for maximum reception.

56

Thoracic Park

If your dog likes to roll over, he may not necessarily be asking for a belly rub. Try a nice chest massage instead.

57

Parlez-Vous Chien?

Try speaking common words or commands in a different language, but use the same vocal inflection as usual. Your dog may actually understand what you mean!

58

Lazy Man's Tetherball

Not feeling particularly
energetic, but still want to offer
entertainment for your dog?
Tie a balloon (just out of reach) to
your ceiling fan, and let it spin.

NOTE: If your dog starts spinning out of control,
this may not be the game for her. Making her dizzy
is not good for her or your carpet!

59

Bobbing for Treats

Toss treats and/or toys into a shallow pool or bucket. Step back and have a mop ready.

60

Blow bubbles.

Lawrence Welk fans found soap bubbles soothing. Your dog probably finds them energizing. Watch her leap and snap.

61

Rub the kneebows.

Take a look at your dog's hocks. They aren't exactly knees; they aren't exactly elbows. Massage this funny, forgotten joint.

62

One More Set

Incorporate your dog into your workout routine by substituting her for your hand weights or dumbbells! Dachshunds (or any dogs with long torsos— so long as their spines are well supported) work well.

63

Blind Spot

Scratch the hard-to-reach spots on the dog. Sometimes our more chubby friends can't reach every itch. They love it when you do.

64

Beam Me Up, Scotty!

For the high-tech dog that is way beyond squeaky toys, invest in a laser pointer. This elusive quarry can jump from wall to wall, and is not bound by the physical laws of conventional balls and toys—something dogs love to hate!

NOTE: Some dogs will ignore the laser, but most develop a deep personal vendetta against their new archenemy.

65

Peanut-Butter Swirl

Place a small amount of peanut butter on your dog's tail and watch her spin like a top. This is great for an antsy dog with boundless energy and restricted space. She'll whirl away her pent-up energy, and if she ever does catch her tail, she'll have a tasty little treat!

66

Shell Game

Play the classic sleight-of-hand
game, using a treat and plastic
cups. Dogs have the slight
advantage of being able to
smell which of the rearranged
cups is hiding the treat, but they
are delighted to find it
all the same.

67

Teach your dog to smile . . . literally!

Start by lifting your dog's lips to inspect his teeth and gums, all the while repeating the word "Smile!" With time, he will curl his lips back on command, and before you know it, you'll truly have a smiling dog.

68

Dogs love when you speak in rhyme.

Compose a poem in honor of your dog's traits or attributes and recite it out loud.

69

Pupsicle

The next time you are preparing
an ice-cube tray, drop a kibble into
each well before it freezes.
How many licks does it take to get
to the surprise nugget inside?

70

Hush-hush

Dogs love a good secret!
Even an ordinary statement takes
on special importance when you
whisper it into your dog's ear.
Watch his reaction when you
come in close to whisper,
"Go for a walk?"

71

"Figaro, Figaro, Figaro!"

Dogs love when you sing opera. Don't worry if you don't speak Italian; your dog will prefer that you change the words and sing about him.

72

"It's a bird, it's a plane!"

Throw on a cape and whirl around the yard like a superhero. Your dog will love being your trusty sidekick and will get a laugh out of your silly outfit.

73

Slow-mo

Dogs are fascinated by extremes. Try performing normal activities, such as preparing a treat, in slow motion. Tremors of anticipation can reach 4.0 on the Richter scale.

74

Call of the Wild

Make it a ritual during each full moon (or any time you feel like it) to join your dog outside for a no-holds-barred howling session. Letting loose with a great howl is a liberating release for both of you.

75

Human Hurdle

Throw a ball or toy into another
room and then crouch down in the
doorway. Once the toy
is retrieved and the dog makes
his jaunt back toward you,
he must leap over the new barrier
in the doorway. Dogs love when
they can jump over you!

76

Bag it.

Hide your dog's favorite toy in
a large brown grocery bag.
Shake the bag provocatively,
and let your dog root out the prize.

77

"Gooaal!"

A ball doesn't need to fit in your dog's mouth to be fun! Many dogs—especially herding breeds— are natural soccer players and can expertly shuffle a large ball about with their front legs or even noses. Many dogs quickly master the keep-away objective of a good game of soccer.

78

Peek-a-boo

Even dogs find the classic game of peek-a-boo entertaining. However, unlike many children, they are not impressed with you merely hiding your face behind your hands (smart dogs). You can achieve much better effects by hiding completely beneath a blanket or sheet. Peek slyly from your hiding place and surreptitiously say her name, but watch out as she dives for your cover.

79

I Got Your Nose!

Grasp your dog's muzzle and quickly pull your cupped hand away, making a popping noise with your mouth. Many dogs get very excited by this game. (Geordie is not sure.)

80

Lord of the Rings

Still have that Hula-Hoop stashed in your garage? Some dogs love to jump through hoops.
Start with the hoop placed low to the ground, and toss a treat through. As your dog gets the idea, you can gradually raise the hoop until your pooch is leaping through the ring.

NOTE: While it is indeed dramatic, your dog will definitely not attempt the circus version of this game with a flaming ring. So don't even think about it!

81

The Raspberry

Okay, so this game is not for everyone. But many dogs are actually tickled by a variation on the classic "raspberry." Place your mouth over an expanse of the dog's skin, for example, near the armpit, then blow! *"Fffppppttt!"*

NOTE: You can even just try sticking out your tongue and making the noise. You may even get it back.

82

Incoming!

Use a slingshot or a spoon to
catapult nuggets of kibble
across the yard for your dog
to pursue!

83

Cultural Heritage

Would your Viszla enjoy a polka? Would your Chihuahua like to hear a mariachi band? Does your poodle appreciate the accordion? Try exposing your dog to music from his native land. If your dog has been reluctant to dance, perhaps it is simply because she didn't know the steps!

84

Piggy-Back Ride

Get down on all fours and coax
your dog—small breeds only,
please!—onto your back
(this may require some help).
Once your dog is comfortable
on her new human perch, crawl
around, transporting your dog
around the house or yard.
This takes "going for a ride"
to a whole new level!

85

Pied Piper

Do you play the flute (or kazoo)?
Can you beat out a rhythm on
a drum? Use any instrument to
call your dog into an impromptu
musical procession, and watch her
follow the leader!

86

Bowl-O-Rama

Line up your dog's toys (stuffed animals work best) into the pyramidal arrangement of bowling pins. You then roll a ball into the group, scattering the toys about and watching the dog try to figure out which to rescue first.

87

Water Taxi

Not every dog is a great swimmer, but that doesn't mean they can't join in the fun. Many dogs will stand or lie on an air mattress, enjoying the pool without getting wet. You may want to try getting your dog to walk on the mattress while it's on solid ground to get her used to the sensation. So much better than being left poolside!

NOTE: Of course, air mattresses and long nails don't mix! And please don't let the dog near water without a lifeguard.

88

Sockie Ball

Looking for something to do with all of those socks that are mysteriously left without their mates after going through the wash? Roll them up and make a soft ball to throw inside the house.

97 Ways to Make a Dog Smile

89

Courier Pigeon

Have a message to send to
someone in another room
of the house? Don't yell—attach a
note to the dog and send him on
the errand: "Go find Daddy!"

90

Everybody Limbo!

Use a broom or mop handle as
a limbo pole, and limbo away!
Be prepared for serious cheating.
Dogs will go under the handle
stomach-down, and when the
going gets tough, they usually
give up and leap over the handle.

91

Hip-Hop

Hop up and down! One foot!
Both feet! Everyone!

92

Leapfrog

Here's a more elaborate variation on the simple hopping routine. Start in a squat or crouch, and spring upward in your best froggie impression. "Ribbits" are optional.

93

Chutes and Ladders

Some dogs will take advantage of the park's playground equipment and shimmy down the children's slide! Smaller dogs may prefer to ride on your lap. Whee!

94

Buried Treasure

Fill a large shallow box or
old kiddie pool with soil, and
bury fun treats and toys in the dirt.
Natural diggers love to have their
own space to root around in.

95

Twist the Night Away

Dogs with short tails seem to be naturally adept at doing the Twist! Lacking a substantial tail, their whole rump wags and wiggles in an exaggerated expression. Pop in a Chubby Checker album and twist away happily with your stub-tailed friend!

96

Patty-Cake

When the dog is lying down, put one of your hands on top of her paws. He will probably pull it away and may put his paw on top of your hand. Then you pull out your hand and put it on top of his paw, and so on.

97

Hot Pursuit

Strap a stuffed animal on top of
a remote-controlled car,
and let 'er rip!

NOTE: This is especially fun for
racing or hunting breeds.

Acknowledgments

This book would not exist without the inspiration of editor par excellence Jennifer Griffin. Her dedication, persistence, patience, and belief in this project were inestimable.

Many thanks also to photographer Pat Doyle, as well as all of the doggie models (and their people!). Their participation made this project not only possible, but happy and fun.

Special thanks to all of my dear friends at Blue Cross Pet Hospital and Lenox Hill Veterinarians.

The gratitude of a lifetime goes to Robby, who loves dogs and cats equally. He never met a person he could not make smile, and he forever holds his mommy's heart.

Photo Credits

Original photography by Pat Doyle.

Front Cover:
Eric Isselée/fotolia

Back Cover:
Andres Rodriguez/fotolia

Additional Stock Photography:
Note: The numbers below refer to the dog number.

jagodka/fotolia 1; Eric Isselée/fotolia 3; Willee Cole/
fotolia 10; cynoclub/fotolia 15; Aseph/shutterstock 21;
Eric Isselée/fotolia 23; Andres Rodriguez/fotolia 28;
Monika Obermajerová/shutterstock 30; cynoclub/
shutterstock 32; Fly_dragonfly/fotolia 45; jagodka/
fotolia 52; Li Kim Goh/iStockphoto 53; jagodka/fotolia
58; Alexia Khruscheva/shutterstock 64; otsphoto/
shutterstock 67; sutichak/fotolia 71; Viorel Sima/fotolia
72; biglama/fotolia 74; Farinoza/fotolia 88; JackF/fotolia
89; Eric Isselée/fotolia 93.

Also in this series:

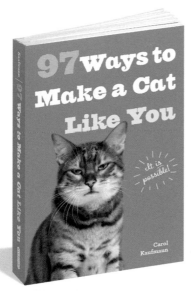

97 WAYS TO MAKE A CAT LIKE YOU

It's the perfect interactive guide to these mysterious, fickle, seemingly aloof— yet, really, just misunderstood— pets, pairing full-color photographs of friendly cats (so owners can recognize what "like" looks like in a cat) with 97 inspired, occasionally silly tips and tricks, all based on cat behavior and biology. Each proves that when a cat is treated right, he or she will respond in kind. Within reason.